SHIPS AND BOATS

Curriculum Consultants

Dr. Arnold L. Willems
Associate Professor of Curriculum and Instruction
The University of Wyoming

Dr. Gerald W. Thompson
Associate Professor
Social Studies Education
Old Dominion University

Dr. Dale Rice
Associate Professor
Department of Elementary and Early Childhood Education
University of South Alabama

Dr. Fred Finley
Assistant Professor of Science Education
University of Wisconsin

Subject Area Consultants

Astronomy
Robert Burnham
Associate Editor
Astronomy Magazine and *Odyssey* Magazine

Geology
Dr. Norman P. Lasca
Professor of Geology
University of Wisconsin — Milwaukee

Oceanography
William MacLeish
Editor
Oceanus Magazine

Paleontology
Linda West
Dinosaur National Monument
Jensen, Utah

Physiology
Kirk Hogan, M.D.
Madison, Wisconsin

Sociology/Anthropology
Dr. Arnold Willems
Associate Professor of Curriculum and Instruction
College of Education
University of Wyoming

Technology
Dr. Robert T. Balmer
Professor of Mechanical Engineering
University of Wisconsin — Milwaukee

Transportation
James A. Knowles
Division of Transportation
Smithsonian Institution

Irving Birnbaum
Air and Space Museum
Smithsonian Institution

Donald Berkebile
Division of Transportation
Smithsonian Institution

Zoology
Dr. Carroll R. Norden
Professor of Zoology
University of Wisconsin —
  Milwaukee

Managing editor
Patricia Daniels

Editors
Herta Breiter
Darlene Shinozaki Kuhnke

Patricia Laughlin
Norman Mysliwiec

Designers
Faulkner/Marks

Jane Palecek

Artists
Fred Anderson
John Barber
John Bilham
Jacky Cowdrey
Chris Flynn
Gilchrist Studios
Elizabeth Graham-Yool
Colin Hawkins

Richard Hook
Illustra
Eric Jewell
Angus McBride
Ann Procter
John Sibbick
Andrew Skilleter
George Thompson

First published by Macmillan Publishers Limited, 1979
Illustrations copyright © Macmillan Publishers Limited
  and Raintree Publishers Inc.
Text copyright © 1981 Raintree Publishers Inc.

Library of Congress Number: 80-22959
1 2 3 4 5 6 7 8 9 84 83 82 81
Printed and bound in the United States of America.

Library of Congress Cataloging in Publication Data
Main entry under title:

Let's discover ships and boats.

  (Let's discover;   )
  Bibliography: p. 67
  Includes index.
  SUMMARY: A reference book dealing with the
small craft of rivers and canals and the large
sailing ships, steamships, warships, and cargo and
passenger ships.
  1. Ships — Juvenile literature. 2. Boats and
boating — Juvenile literature. [1. Ships.
2. Boats and boating] I. Title: Ships and
boats. II. Series.
AG6.L43   [VM150]   013s [623.8'2]
ISBN 0-8172-1774-6   80-22959

LET'S DISCOVER
SHIPS AND BOATS

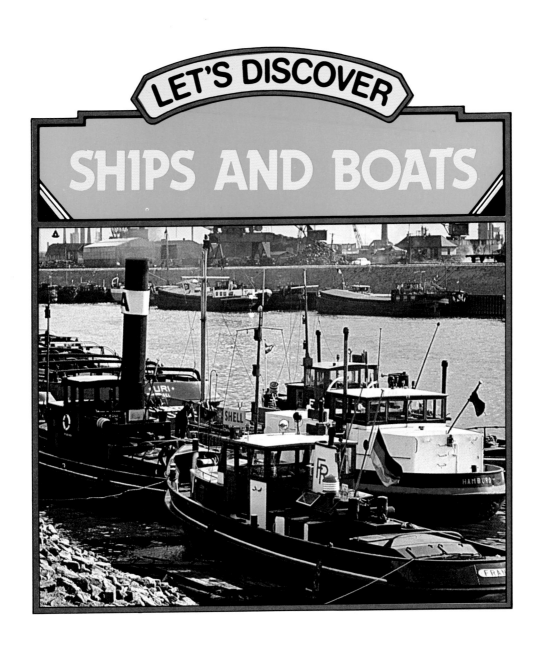

RAINTREE PUBLISHERS
Milwaukee • Toronto • Melbourne • London

Contents

SMALL BOATS — 6

The first boats — 8

Simple boats today — 10

RIVERS AND CANALS — 12

Travel by river — 14

How a canal works — 16

Canals — 18

SAILING SHIPS — 20

Oars and sails — 22

Galleons and cogs — 24

Life on board ship — 26

Clipper ships — 28

Tall ships — 30

Modern sailing boats — 32

STEAMSHIPS — 34

The Great Britain — 36

Battleships — 38

CARGO SHIPS — 40

Modern cargo ships — 42

Tankers — 44

Shipbuilding —————————————— 46

PASSENGER SHIPS ————————————— 48
   Liners ——————————————————— 49
   Ferries —————————————————— 50
   Hydrofoils ————————————————— 52
   Hovercraft ————————————————— 53

MODERN WARSHIPS —————————— 54
   Naval activities ———————————————— 56
   Submarines ————————————————— 58

UNUSUAL SHIPS —————————————— 60
   Ships for special purposes ————————— 62

GLOSSARY ———————————————— 64

FURTHER READING ————————————— 67

QUESTIONS TO THINK ABOUT —————— 69

PROJECTS ————————————————— 76

INDEX ——————————————————— 77

SMALL BOATS

Many people use small boats for fun. Some boats are rowed with oars or paddles. Some boats have sails. Other kinds of boats have engines. People learn how to use their boats before they go on the water.

sailing boat

speedboat

motorboat

Many boats are too big to take home. They are kept in boathouses or in special harbors. An inflatable boat can be taken home. All the air is let out of it first.

inflatable boat

rowboat

The first boats

People learned to float down rivers on logs long before they rode horses or made carts. This hunter has tied two logs together. He paddles with his hands.

Later, people made better boats called dugouts. They used fire and stone axes to hollow out tree trunks.

This raft is made of tree trunks tied together. The paddle helps to steer the boat.

This fine sailing ship was built about 5,000 years ago. The float, fixed to poles called outriggers, kept it from blowing over.

float

Simple boats today

Simple sailing boats in Asia are called junks. Junks have flat bottoms.

We can see all these boats today. They have been made the same way for hundreds of years. They are used for fishing, for travel, and for carrying cargoes.

In some parts of South America the jungle is very thick. There are no roads, so people travel along the rivers. This longboat is used in Peru.

This picture was taken in Hong Kong. The land is very crowded, so many people live on their boats.

Coracles are small boats for one person. They are covered with stretched animal skins. They are used for fishing.

Many simple boats are made of bundles of reeds tied together. These reed boats are on Lake Titicaca in South America.

RIVERS AND CANALS

Canals are waterways made by people. They are straighter than rivers and wide enough for large boats and barges. Most canals were built long ago, when roads were bad and few railways had been built.

The tugs and barges below are on the Rhine River in Germany. There is more river traffic on the Rhine than on any other river in the world.

Long ago, horses pulled heavy loads. It often took as many as six horses to pull a wagon.

The same heavy load could be put on a barge and pulled along a canal by one horse.

Rivers and canals sometimes go in different directions. This canal was built higher than the river that flows under the bridge.

Travel by River

Rivers have been used for travel for a long time. The Nile is the most important river in Egypt. This boat was built by the Egyptians 5,000 years ago. Boats like this carried people and cargoes.

Egyptian ships are the oldest ships we know about. Some of the earliest ships had a mast like the letter A. This ship has one mast and a long rectangular sail. The large oar at the stern, or back, was used for steering.

The other boats shown are galleys. They were rowed by teams of men pulling oars.

15

How a canal works

When a canal is built on sloping land it must be made like a series of steps. The different levels of the steps are joined by locks. Locks are pairs of gates. When they are shut, no water can get in or out.

Locks have gates at each end. A boat enters through one gate. Water is then slowly run into or out of the lock through sluices. When the boat has been raised or lowered to the right level, it can leave by the other gate.

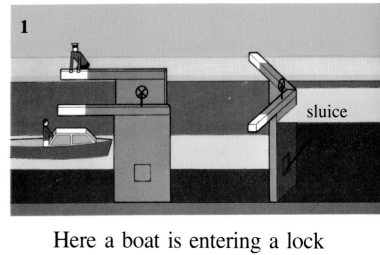

Here a boat is entering a lock from the lower level. The top gate is kept shut.

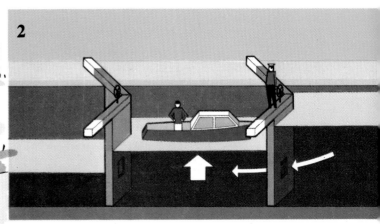

The lower gate closes. Water from the top sluice raises the boat. Then the top gate opens.

Amsterdam, in The Netherlands, has many beautiful canals. This boat is taking people on a trip along a canal.

Canals

Most canals link towns and cities. Some have other uses. Sometimes a canal is dug through a narrow part of the land to join two seas together. Other canals are inside cities. They are used instead of streets.

It was hard work building canals. The people who built them were sometimes called navvies.

This is the Corinth Canal in Greece. It was cut through land to join two seas together. Sea canals made voyages shorter. People no longer had to sail around the land.

Venice, in Italy, has canals instead of streets. Boats called gondolas are used instead of cars. Gondolas take people where they want to go. Some people in Venice need a boat to get next door!

SAILING SHIPS

Thousands of years ago people learned that a ship could be driven along by the wind pushing against a sail.

At first ships could only go where the wind blew them. Then new kinds of sails were made that could be swung from side to side. Ships could then go in any direction. To sail directly into the wind they had to go in a zigzag.

Modern sails are curved. Wind blowing over the curve lifts the sail. Blow over a sheet of paper and watch it lift.

20

When a boat sails into a strong wind the crew have to lean out as far as they can. This keeps the boat from being blown over.

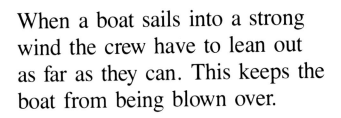

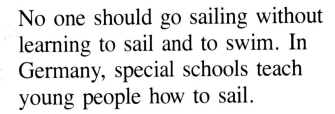

No one should go sailing without learning to sail and to swim. In Germany, special schools teach young people how to sail.

Vikings from the North sailed in ships like this 1,000 years ago. They raided Britain, France, and other places. They sailed across the Atlantic.

Oars and sails

Galleys were large ships rowed by many men. They moved much faster than ships that had only sails. When there was no wind, sailing ships hardly moved at all. Pirates used galleys to overtake slower sailing ships.

The Arabs invented the lateen sail 1,000 years ago. Their boats could sail into the wind.

lateen sail

22

This Greek galley is like the
Egyptian ships built 5,000 years
ago. It had a pointed metal bow
to smash into enemy ships.
There are two rows of oars.
Some galleys had even more
rows of oars. The soldiers used
shields to protect themselves.

Galleons and cogs

About 600 years ago most ships had sails but no oars. Galleons were the largest ships. They had three or four masts rigged with many sails. Cogs were simple cargo ships with wide hulls and one mast.

A crow's nest was set at the top of the mast. From there a sailor could watch for land or for other ships.

Sailors had to fight pirates sometimes. They fought from the high decks at each end of the ship.

high foredeck

hull

high poop deck

By about 500 years ago merchant ships were able to make long voyages. Their country's flag was flown at the top of the mast.

Life on board ship

In the old days there were no canned foods or refrigerators. Crews often became ill because they had no fresh vegetables or fruit to eat. There was little fresh water to drink.

Sailors had to climb masts in dreadful storms. The ships tossed from side to side. Ropes and sails flapped about in the wind.

Life on board the sailing ships was hard. Voyages might take a year or more. Sailors were cramped together, and the work was tiring. Sailors were often cross and unhappy.

The hardest and most dangerous work was hauling up the sails and letting them down. Sailors had to climb rope ladders to the tops of the masts.

In the old days, the crew slept on the hard deck or in a hammock. A hammock was a bed of netting or canvas. It was unrolled each night and slung from a hook at each end.

When a galleon met a strong storm, its sails had to be taken down. A strong wind could snap a mast or tear the sails to shreds.

Sailors used a capstan to pull heavy ropes. A capstan was like a drum with poles sticking out from it. The capstan turned as the sailors pushed the poles around. They sang songs to keep together as they moved around the capstan.

Many clipper ships had carved figureheads on their bows. They were meant to bring luck.

Clipper ships

Clipper ships were the fastest sailing ships. They sped across the world with trading goods. They were long, narrow ships with several masts and many sails. Clipper ships needed a large crew.

One of the most famous clipper ships was the Cutty Sark. It is shown at the right. The Cutty Sark is now kept on the Thames River in England.

Clipper ships sometimes raced each other. Over a hundred years ago two clipper ships had a race all the way from China to England. The American ships, or "Yankee clippers," were the fastest of all.

Tall ships

Large sailing ships that carried cargoes about a hundred years ago are called tall ships. There were two kinds of tall ships, barks and schooners. Barks usually had three masts. Schooners had two masts. Both barks and schooners had many sails.

Some tall ships are used today for training sailors. Life on a modern training ship is often as tough and as dangerous as in the old days.

This is a training-school sailing ship. This bark has three masts and lots of sails.

Viking boat

galleon

Modern sailing boats

Most of today's sailing boats are used for sport. Most of them are small. They do not go very far from land. A few larger sailing ships are used for ocean racing. Some can go around the world.

Life on an ocean racer is exciting. The crew must work together to sail well.

This boat is called a yawl. It has a huge front sail called a spinnaker. This big sail makes the boat go very fast.

full rigged ship

modern sailing boat

Sails have changed a lot over the years. At first, ships were made to go faster by adding more masts and sails. Today's fast racers usually have only one mast.

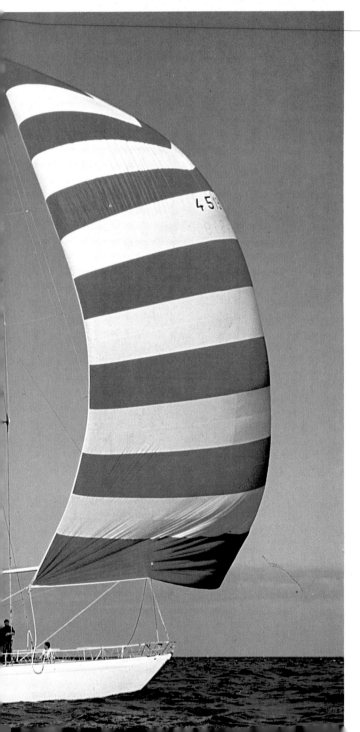

One of the world's fastest racers is called Crossbow. It has two hulls, side by side. Each hull has its own mast.

galleon

bark

paddle
steamer

steamship

passenger liner

Steamships developed gradually from sailing ships. For many years they kept their sails because their engines often broke down.

Steamships

All the earliest steamships had paddle wheels. There was usually a wheel on each side.

Paddle wheels were like old water wheels. They were driven by the ship's engine. As they turned round and round, they pushed the boat along the water.

The stern-wheeler had a large wheel at the back. It was used on rivers too narrow for ships with side-wheels.

This paddle steamer is in Disney World in Florida. It is a copy of a stern-wheeler used long ago on the Mississippi.

The Great Britain

This ship, the Great Britain, was finished in 1843. At first it had paddle wheels. Then the paddle wheels were taken off and a screw propeller was put on.

The Great Britain was one of the biggest ships of its time. It was made of iron rather than wood. It made its first trip from England to New York in fifteen days.

Battleships

For a long time, battleships were the biggest warships. They had heavy guns and thick armor. Battleships were first used in a war over a hundred years ago.

gun turrets

In 1906 Great Britain built the Dreadnought. It had its large guns placed in turrets. The turrets turned so that the guns could be moved from side to side as they fired.

Other countries copied the Dreadnought. Many giant battleships were built. Today other types of ships are used instead of battleships.

One of the last battleships was the USS Alabama. It was built at the end of World War Two. The United States used some battleships until 1970.

CARGO SHIPS

Hundreds of years ago, ships took people from Europe to settle in North America. The ships brought goods back to Europe. The cargoes included things like corn, potatoes, and tobacco. These goods had never been seen before in Europe.

In the old days, a ship's cargo included many different things. Flour, wine, animals, timber, and other things were all mixed up together. It took a long time to load and unload the barrels, crates, and loose cargo such as coal. It was very tiring work.

Modern cargo ships

Today the way of moving cargo has changed. Ships carry either bulk or container cargo. Coal and oil are bulk cargoes. They are poured into the hold or sucked out quickly by machines. Cargoes such as furniture, books, and cars are packed in containers.

Grain, such as wheat and oats, does not have to be put into sacks. It is loaded and unloaded through big pipes.

Coffee is usually packed in sacks. Cranes lift many sacks at the same time.

Containers are made to fit exactly in certain parts of a cargo ship.

Oil is the most important bulk cargo. It travels in special ships called tankers.

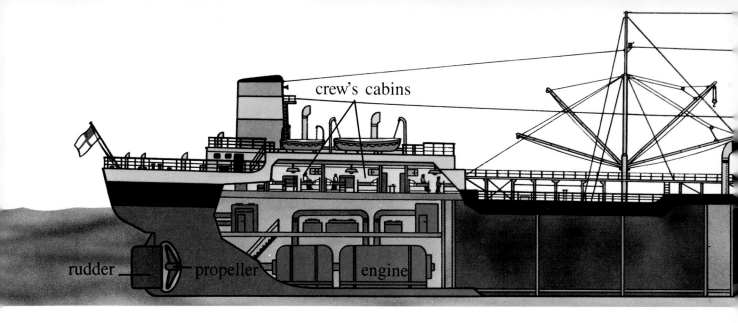

crew's cabins

rudder — propeller — engine

Tankers

In the past years, oil tankers have become bigger and bigger. Today they are the biggest ships in the world. They have grown in size so they can carry more oil on one trip. This lowers the cost of shipping it. The oil is held in large tanks in the center of the ship.

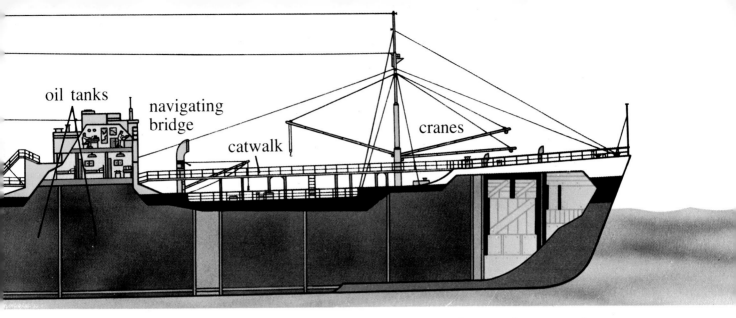

oil tanks

navigating bridge

catwalk

cranes

A tanker's engines and crew cabins are at the stern. Some tankers have a navigating bridge near the center. Ships are steered from the bridge.

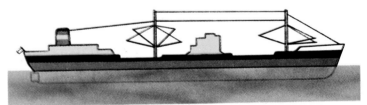

When its tanks are empty, the tanker rides high. Most of its great hull is out of the water.

A tanker's hull is usually painted in two colors. The part above water is gray or black. The underside is red.

On the biggest tankers, the crew use bicycles to go from one part of the deck to another. It is a long walk from the bow to the stern of a tanker.

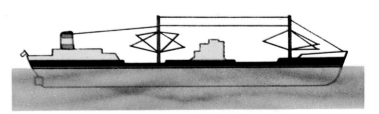

As a tanker is filled, it sinks deeper into the water. Most of the hull is under the water.

Shipbuilding

Today, large parts of ships are made in factories. The parts are then brought to a dock. There, they are put into place by giant cranes and joined together. This makes the outdoor work quicker.

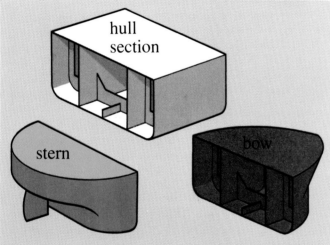

Some shipbuilders use the same kind of large parts for all of their ships.

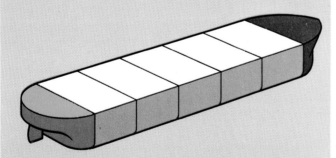

Sections are joined together in the right order to make a complete ship. The entire job can be done in a few months.

PASSENGER SHIPS

Liners

Passenger ships called liners were once the only way people could cross the sea to different places. Now airplanes can carry people much faster. Most liners now are used for vacation cruises. Liners are like big floating hotels. They have restaurants, pools, game rooms, and movies. People can have lots of fun on board.

Ferries

A ferry is a boat that travels between two places close together. Some ferries take people across a river where there is no bridge. Others travel across a bay or a lake. The fastest ferries are new ships called hydrofoils.

The picture at the right shows the Star Ferry in Hong Kong. Many people use it every day.

Small ferries are pulled over a river by hauling on a rope stretched from bank to bank.

In some places there is not enough traffic for people to want to build a bridge. A ferry can take care of all the people who want to cross.

Some ferries carry cars and trucks. You can drive straight on board at one side and drive off when the ferry has crossed the water.

Train ferries have rails on their decks. The train cars are pushed aboard and carried across the water. The train may be full of passengers asleep in beds!

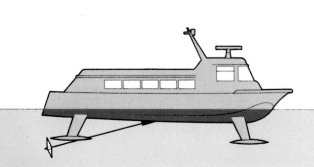

At anchor, the hydrofoil rests in the water like other boats.

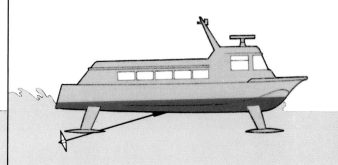

As it moves forward, it begins to rise up on its lifting foils.

Hydrofoils

A hydrofoil is a boat that rides above the water. It is supported on small "water wings" called foils. It can move much faster than ordinary ships. Hydrofoils can be more steady than other ships in rough weather.

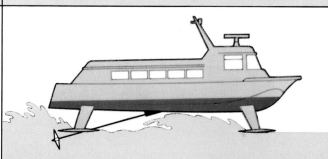

At full speed, the foils keep the hull completely above water. Hydrofoils can move very fast.

Hovercraft

These craft are sometimes called air-cushion craft. They are supported by a cushion of air pumped in below. Most Hovercraft are used over water, but they can also travel on land. They can move over soft mud and snow.

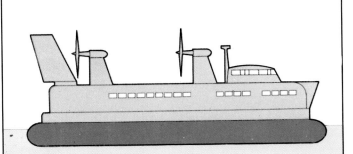

When still, a Hovercraft lies in the water like ordinary ships.

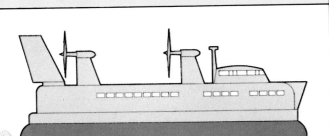

When the engines start, the craft rises on its cushion of air and skims across the waves.

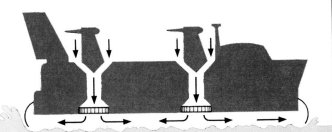

The engines drive big fans. The fans suck in air and blow it into the cushion.

destroyer

MODERN WARSHIPS

Today's warships still have guns and armor like the old warships. But many things are new about them. Crews are much smaller. Many jobs are done by machines worked by computers.

Cruisers and destroyers are two kinds of warships. Destroyers are smaller than cruisers and can move very fast. Both have big guns.

cruiser

aircraft carrier

Aircraft carriers are the biggest warships. Airplanes can take off and land on their huge decks.

cruiser

helicopter carrier

Some cruisers have nuclear engines. They carry missiles to fire at enemy aircraft and submarines.

A new kind of ship is both a helicopter carrier and an anti-submarine cruiser.

submarines

Today's nuclear-powered submarines can stay underwater for months at a time. Some carry long-range missiles.

frigate

Frigates can do many jobs. They have anti-submarine missiles and guns. They often have a helicopter too.

Naval activities

In the old days, hundreds of sailors worked on a small ship. Today, computers do many of the jobs sailors used to do.

Crews are smaller. Naval crews are all experts at their jobs. They are much better paid than sailors used to be.

A captain is still in charge of the ship.

This object is a paravane. It is put into the sea and towed by the ships. Paravanes blow up mines or cut them free to make the sea safe for ships.

At one time, many sailors worked in a noisy and dirty engine room. Today, there is very little work to be done at all in an engine room.

Modern warships use radar for navigating. Radar can find aircraft or other ships even in fog or at night. Objects show up on a radar screen.

Meals are prepared in the galley. The cooks have all the things you would find in the kitchen of a modern hotel.

Submarines

Submarines are boats that can dive and travel under the water. Early submarines were strange objects, like the one below. By about 1900, people could make submarines that could dive under the sea safely.

A canvas bell was one of the first submarines. It was lowered and raised on a rope.

Two hundred years ago an American made a submarine called the Turtle. He used it to sink British ships.

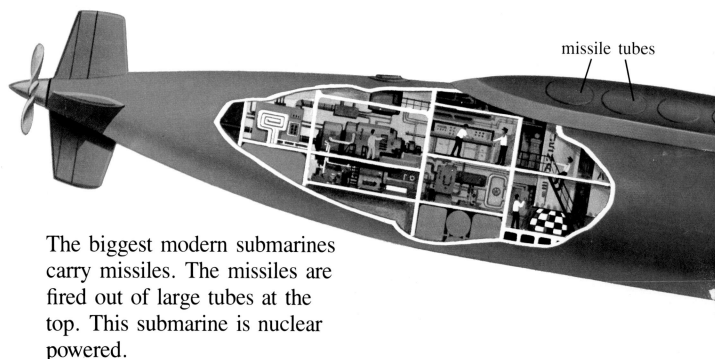

missile tubes

The biggest modern submarines carry missiles. The missiles are fired out of large tubes at the top. This submarine is nuclear powered.

Submarines, like this American one, can also travel on the surface of the water. If there was a war it could stay hidden under the water for a long time.

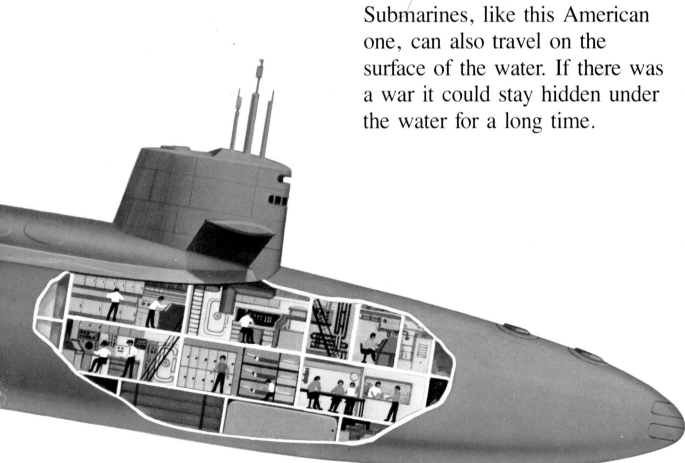

UNUSUAL SHIPS

Over the years, people have built many different kinds of strange ships. The ship with the swan was called a velocipede. It was built in Boston. You made it move by turning a water wheel with your feet.

The "cigar ship" below was not supposed to roll from side to side like other ships. But it rolled very badly.

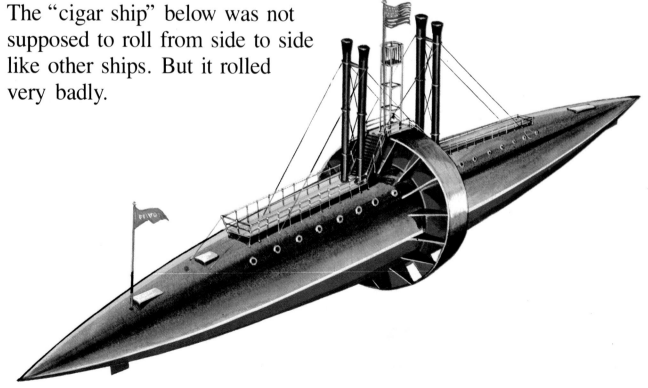

This Russian battleship was
called the Admiral Popoff. It was
round so that it could fire its
guns in any direction. It did not
work very well.

The Connector was hinged so
that it could bend up and down
with the waves.

Ships for special purposes

Many jobs need special kinds of ships and boats. One of the strangest ships can tilt up into the air so that its bow points down into the sea. It is used by people who study life in the ocean.

Fireboats are used to put out fires in buildings near the water. Their powerful engines pump up the water and shoot it out through hoses.

A pontoon is a flat-bottomed boat used to support something. When a bridge has to be built in a hurry it can be built over a row of pontoons. The army often uses pontoon bridges. They can be carried easily.

Ships that sail to the North Pole or South Pole must be very strong. They have to move through thick ice.

Dredgers are fitted with many scoops on a long belt or chain. They scoop out sand and mud from canals, rivers, or harbors. Dredging keeps other ships from getting stuck.

GLOSSARY

These words are defined the way they are used in the book.

aircraft carrier (AIR kraft KAIR ee uhr) a warship with a flat deck on which airplanes can land and take off

barge (bahrj) a boat with a flat bottom, used to carry cargo on rivers and canals

bark (bahrk) a ship with three masts

battleship (BAT uhl shihp) a large warship with many weapons

bow (bow) the front end of a ship

bridge (brihj) a high place on a ship, from which it is steered

bulk (buhlk) a shapeless mass of material

canal (kuh NAL) a waterway built by people to sail on

capstan (KAP stuhn) a drum-like machine used to pull heavy ropes

cargo (KAHR goh) goods that are carried in a ship

clipper (KLIHP uhr) a large, fast sailing ship

cog (kahg) a cargo ship with a wide hull and one mast

computer (kuhm PYOOT uhr) a machine that can store information and can solve problems quickly

container (kuhn TAYN uhr) a covering that holds things in, such as a box or barrel

coracle (KOHR uh kuhl) a small boat made with animal skins

crane (krayn) a tall machine used for lifting heavy things

crow's nest (krohz nehst) a platform high up on a ship's mast, used as a lookout

cruiser (KROOZ uhr) a medium-sized warship

destroyer (dih STROY uhr) a small, fast warship

dredger (DREHJ uhr) a boat used to dig out deeper waterways

dugout (DUHG owt) a boat made by hollowing out a log

engine (EHN juhn) a machine that changes energy into movement

factory (FAK tuh ree) a building or set of buildings where things are made

ferry (FEHR ee) a boat that carries cars or trains across water

figurehead (FIHG yuhr hehd) a carved figure on a ship's bow

galleon (GAL ee uhn) a very large sailing ship with three or four masts

galley (GAL ee) a low ship of the Middle Ages moved by sails and oars; also the name for the kitchen in a ship

gondola (GAHN duh luh) a long,

narrow boat used on canals in Venice, Italy

hammock (HAM uhk) a swinging bed made of cloth and hung up by cords at each end

harbor (HAHR buhr) a protected body of water where ships can anchor

helicopter (HEHL uh kahp tuhr) an aircraft that is held in the air by turning blades on top

Hovercraft (HUHV uhr kraft) a boat that travels on a cushion of air

hull (huhl) the main body of a ship

hydrofoil (HY druh foyl) a boat with fins that lift it away from the water

inflatable (ihn FLAYT uh buhl) able to be puffed up with air

junk (juhngk) a Chinese boat with tall masts

lateen sail (luh TEEN sayl) a sail shaped like a triangle that can move with the wind

liner (LY nuhr) a large ship that carries passengers across the ocean

lock (lahk) a closed-in area on a canal that is used to raise or lower boats from one area to another

mast (mast) a long pole, rising from a ship, that holds the sail

merchant ship (MUHR chuhnt shihp) a ship that carries goods to be sold

mine (myn) a bomb that floats in the water

navigate (NAV uh gayt) to find your way while traveling on the water

nuclear (NOO klee uhr) getting power by the splitting of atoms

outrigger (OWT rihg uhr) an extra fin attached to the side of a boat to keep it steady

paddle wheel (PAD uhl hweel) a wheel with flat boards around its edge, used to move a boat

paravane (PAR uh vayn) a device that is towed underwater by ships to get rid of mines

pontoon (pahn TOON) a boat with a flat bottom used to build floating bridges

propeller (pruh PEHL uhr) a twisted blade that is turned by a ship's engine to push the ship through the water

radar (RAY dar) a device used to find faraway things using radio waves

raft (raft) a flat wood platform that floats on water

sail (sayl) a cloth that catches the wind to push a boat through water

schooner (SKOO nuhr) a large sailing ship with two masts

sluice (sloos) water that is kept behind a gate on a canal

spinnaker (SPIHN ih kuhr) a large sail that is set on the front of a ship

steamship (STEEM shihp) a boat whose engine is moved by steam

stern (stuhrn) the rear end of a boat

stern-wheeler (stuhrn HWEE luhr) a steamboat with a wheel at the stern instead of the sides

submarine (suhb muh REEN) a boat that travels under the water

tanker (TANG kuhr) a cargo boat that has tanks for carrying liquids

turret (TUHR uht) a structure on warships that holds one or more guns

velocipede (vuh LAHS uh peed) a light boat that is moved by pedals

Viking (VY kihng) a northern European pirate of the eighth to tenth centuries

warship (WAWR shihp) a ship used for fighting wars

yawl (yahl) a sailboat with one main mast and a smaller mast in back

FURTHER READING

Adkins, Jan. *Wooden Ship*. Boston: Houghton Mifflin, 1978. 47pp.

Atkinson, I. *The Viking Ships*. New York: Cambridge University Press, 1979.

Benson, Brian. *Ships*. New York: Grosset and Dunlap, 1971. 48pp.

Bowman, Gerald. *Let's Look at Ships*. Chicago: A. Whitman, 1965.

Briggs, Peter. *Science Ship: A Voyage Aboard the Discoverer*. New York: Simon and Schuster, 1969.

Brownlee, W. D. *The First Ships Around the World*. Minneapolis, Minnesota: Lerner Publications Company, 1977. 51pp.

Burchard, Peter. *Ocean Race: A Sea Venture*. New York: G. P. Putnam's and Sons, 1978.

Campbell, Ann R. *Let's Find Out About Boats*. New York: F. Watts, Inc., 1967.

Canright, David. *Ships and the River*. New York: South St. Sea Museum, 1975.

Colby, C. B. *Sailing Ships: Great Ships Before the Age of Steam*. New York: Coward, 1970.

Colby, C. B. *Ships of Commerce: Liners, Tankers, Freighters, Floating Grain Elevators, Tugboats*. New York: Coward, 1963.

Colby, C. B. *Two Centuries of Sea Power*. New York: Coward, 1976. 48pp.

Elting, Mary. *Ships at Work*. rev. ed. New York: Harvey House, 1962. 92pp.

Fenner, Sal. *Sea Machines*. Milwaukee: Raintree Publishers, 1980. 31pp.

Fisher, Leonard E. *Shipbuilders*. New York: F. Watts, Inc., 1971. 48pp.

Goetz, Delia. *Rivers*. New York: William Morrow and Company, Inc., 1969.

Gregor, Hugh. *Warships*. Morristown, New Jersey: Silver Burdett Company, 1979.

Harris, Susan. *Boats and Ships*. New York: F. Watts, Inc., 1979. 48pp.

McCague, James. *When Clipper Ships Ruled the Sea*. New Canaan, Connecticut: Garrard Publishing Company, 1968.

Naden, Corinne J. *The First Book of Rivers*. New York: F. Watts, Inc., 1967. 73pp.

Navarra, John Gabriel. *Superboats*. New York: Doubleday, 1977. 79pp.

Plowden, David. *Tugboat*. New York: Macmillan, 1976. 80pp.

Russell, Solveig P. *The Big Ditch Waterways: The Story of Canals*. New York: Parents Magazine Press, 1977.

Rutland, Jonathan. *See Inside a Galleon*. New York: Warwick Press, 1978. 29pp.

Rutland, Jonathan. *Ships*. New York: Warwick Press, 1976. 47pp.

Wiesenthal, Eleanor, and Ted Wiesenthal. *Let's Find Out About Rivers*. New York: F. Watts, Inc., 1971.

Zim, Herbert, and James Skelly. *Cargo Ships*. New York: William Morrow and Company, 1970. 64pp.

QUESTIONS TO THINK ABOUT

Small Boats

Do you remember?

What are some different kinds of small boats?

What was the first thing people used for traveling on water?

How were dugout boats made?

When was the first sailing ship made?

What is a junk?

How many people can travel in a coracle?

Why do many people in South America have to travel in boats?

Find out about . . .

Early boats. What were some of the early boats like? Who made them? How were they made? What were they used for?

Canoes. How does a canoe differ from other boats? Who made and used canoes? How are they made? Where are they used today?

Outriggers. What are outriggers? How are they different from other boats? What different kinds of outriggers are there? Where are they used?

Rivers and Canals

Do you remember?

What is a canal?

When were most canals made?

What is the world's busiest river?

What were two kinds of ships used by the Egyptians?

What are canal locks used for?

What is a sluice?

Which two cities have many canals?

What did workers called navvies do?

Find out about . . .

River travel. What is the biggest river near you? What kind of boats or ships travel on it? What do they carry? Do people use boats for fun there?

The St. Lawrence Seaway. What is the St. Lawrence Seaway? Where is it? When was it built? Why was it built? How is it used?

The Panama Canal. Who built the Panama Canal? Where is it? When was it built? How long did it take to build it?

Sailing Ships

Do you remember?

Who were the Vikings? What did they do?

Who invented the lateen sail? Why was the lateen sail better than other sails?

What is a galley? What could a galley do that other sailing ships could not do?

What were galleons? How many masts did they have?

What was a crow's nest used for? Where was it placed?

What were the fastest sailing ships?

What are tall ships? What are they used for today?

Find out about . . .

Old warships. How were battles fought at sea in sailing ships? What were some of the famous sea battles? What kinds of ships were used?

Clipper ships. When were clipper ships built? What were they used for? Where did they sail? How fast were they? What were some of the best known clipper ships?

Steamships

Do you remember?

What did all the earliest steamships have?

What was a stern-wheeler?

Why did the early steamships have sails?

What was unusual about the ship Great Britain?

How did battleships differ from other ships?

What was new about the battleship
Dreadnought?

When did the United States stop using
battleships?

Find out about . . .

Steamships. When were steamships first built?
Who made some of the first steamships?
What problems did the early builders have?
What did people think about the first
steamships?

The Merrimack and the Monitor. What were
these two ships built for? What did they look
like? When were they used? What happened
when they met?

The Dreadnought. How big was the
Dreadnought? When was it built? Where did
it fight?

Cargo Ships

Do you remember?

What are two types of cargo ships today?

How is grain loaded and unloaded?

How are things like furniture and books packed
for shipping?

What is the most important bulk cargo?

What are the biggest ships in the world?

What is a navigating bridge used for?

What color is the underside of a tanker painted?

How are many large cargo ships built today?

Find out about . . .

Port cities. Cargo ships dock at cities with ports and harbors. What are some of the important port cities in this country? Where are they?

Oil tankers. How big are modern tankers? How much oil can they carry? Where do many of them sail from? What route do they follow? Where are many of them built?

Passenger Ships

Do you remember?

What are most liners used for today?

What are some of the things you can find on a passenger liner?

What are ferries used for?

Name three things that are carried by ferries.

Where is the Star Ferry?

What is a hydrofoil? How does it work?

What is a hovercraft? How does it work?

What kind of ship can also travel on land?

Find out about . . .

Passenger liners. What are some of the most

famous passenger liners? When were they built? What are they used for? Where do they sail? How many people can they carry?

Hydrofoils and hovercraft. Where are these kinds of craft used? When were they first built? How fast can they travel?

Modern Warships

Do you remember?

What are the largest warships?

Which is larger, a cruiser or a destroyer?

Which is faster, a cruiser or a destroyer?

What kind of ships carry missiles?

Why do modern warships need smaller crews?

What is a paravane used for?

Why do modern ships use radar?

When was the first submarine built?

What was the Turtle? When was it made?

Find out about . . .

Warships. What are some different kinds of modern warships? Find out about each kind. How big is it? What kinds of weapons does it have? How big is its crew? How long can it stay at sea?

The U.S. Navy. How many people serve in the

Navy? Who can join the Navy? What are some of the kinds of work people in the Navy are trained to do? What are some of the good things about serving in the Navy?

Unusual Ships

Do you remember?

What was the velocipede? What made it move across the water?

What was the "cigar ship" not supposed to do?

Why was the Admiral Popoff built in a strange shape?

What was unusual about the Connector?

What are pontoons used for?

What are dredgers used for?

Find out about . . .

First trips. Who made the first trip to the North Pole? To the South Pole? Who were the first people to sail to North America? Who made the first voyage eastward from Europe to India?

Unusual ships. Find out about other kinds of unusual ships or boats. What is unusual about them? Why were they built? Who built them? When?

PROJECTS

Project — Fun with Words

Some words have more than one meaning. A galley is a boat pulled by many oars. A galley is also a kitchen on board a ship. Many of the words in this book have more than one meaning.

Take a sheet of paper and divide it into two columns. Write the heading SHIP AND BOAT MEANINGS at the top of the first column. Write OTHER MEANINGS at the top of the other column. Then use a dictionary for help. Find at least two meanings for each of these words:

junk	bridge	cog
bark	turret	bow
stern	foil	tug

Write the ship and boat meanings in the first column. Write the other meanings in the second column.

Project — Building a Model Ship

You can make a small model of a ship with sticks, scraps of wood, paper boxes, scraps of cloth, or other things you can find around the house. Find a book in the library that will show you how to make a model ship. The book will tell you what materials you can use. It will show you how to build your model.

INDEX

Aircraft carriers 55
Barges 12
Barks 30-31
Battleships 38-39
Bulk cargo 42, 43
Canals 12-13, 16-19
Capstan 27
Cargo ships 40-41
Clipper ships 28-29
Cogs 25
Container cargo 42, 43
Coracles 11
Cruisers 54, 55
Cutty Sark 28
Destroyers 54
Dreadnought 38
Dredgers 63
Dugouts 8
Ferries 50-51
Fireboats 62
Flags 24, 25
Frigates 55
Galleons 24, 26
Galleys 15, 22-23
Hovercraft 53
Hydrofoils 50, 52
Inflatable boats 7
Junks 10
Lateen sail 22
Liners 48-49
Locks 16-17
Longboats 10
Ocean racers 32, 33
Paddle wheels 34-35

Passenger ships 48-49
Pontoons 62
Radar 57
Rafts 9
Reed boats 11
Rigging 30
Sailing ships 9, 20-21, 26, 30
Schooners 30
Sea canals 19
Shipbuilding 46
Sluices 17
Steamships 34
Stern-wheeler 35
Submarines 55, 58-59
Tall ships 30-31
Tankers 43-45
The Great Britain 36-37
Training ships 30
Tugs 12
Warships 38, 54-55
Yachts 32
Yawls 32

Photo Credits:
British Tourist Authority; Douglas Dickins, F.R.P.S.;
Jonathan Eastland; Robert Harding Associates; Michael
Holford; Leo Mason; Overseas Containers Ltd.;
Picturepoint; Shell Oil; Zefa.
Cover: Wide World Photos